The Power of Positive Thinking

A Self-Help Guide on How to Overcome Negativity, Adversity, Depression, and Change Your Life

by Michael Dyer

© 2016 Michael Dyer
All Rights Reserved

Table of Contents

The Power of Positive Thinking

Table of Contents

Introduction

Chapter 1- Changing Your Story

Chapter 2- Time Out

Chapter 3- The Placebo Effect

The Way Forward

Disclaimer

While all attempts have been made to verify the information provided in this book, the author does not assume any responsibility for errors, omissions, or contrary interpretations of the subject matter contained within. The information provided in this book is for educational and entertainment purposes only. The reader is responsible for his or her own actions and the author does not accept any responsibilities for any liabilities or damages, real or perceived, resulting from the use of this information.

Introduction

"The greatest discovery of all time is that a person can change his future by merely changing his attitude." ~ Oprah Winfrey

The mind is one of the great mysteries of the universe. Neurosurgeons, psychologists, psychiatrists, sociologists, artists, writers, painters, even businessmen study it for various reasons.

Whether they're assisting a patient heal, painting a portrait of a forlorn woman, crafting a sculpture of a man thinking, developing a character for a novel that tugs on the heartstrings, performing lifesaving surgery, or gaining a tactical advantage in a negotiation, we ultimately want to know why people do what they do, say what they say, and act the way they act.

What compels us?
What inspires us?
Most importantly, what defeats us and how can we overcome those setbacks?

Marcus Aurelius, the great ancient Roman emperor contemplated this very problem two thousand years ago. Today, we still argue over it. He put it most succinctly when he said, "You have power over your mind – not outside events. Realize this, and you will find strength."

It is within ourselves to write our own destiny. That power has always resided within. What holds us back? What holds you back from achieving your dreams? Setting out on the path that you know is true for your life?

Our inside voice is filled with self-doubt, and negative self-talk. We seem compelled, as a people, to talk ourselves out of doing things rather than encouraging our development. The simple fact is it's easier to be negative than to be positive.

If you have a dream to start a business, your mind immediately fills with doubts. I've never written a business plan, I don't have money to invest in it, I don't have time to devote to it, who will I get to fund my idea?

These kinds of ideas take shape in our head and are difficult to remove. Before you know it, it could quickly spiral out of control, leading you to an unfortunate conclusion. Anger, resentment, anxiety, even depression loom on the horizon.

JAMES

Many years ago I knew a man. For anonymity purposes, we'll call him James. He was bright, articulate, graduated from a prestigious university whereupon he was offered a position at a law firm as an attorney. For years, James thrived. Until one day, things changed.

James grew up in a small household. His mother was a social worker, his father, a gifted engineer. James was scarred as a child by his mother. Over a career of seeing the worst aspects of families in our society, she was bitter and took her frustration out on James.

His life was a quest to please her. Hoping to aspire to more than what she'd seen over the course of working with abused children from dysfunctional families. Little did she know, she was creating discord within her own home.

Despite his stunning academic achievements, his high salary, his multi-million dollar house, his mother's negativity stuck with him, burrowed in the deep recesses of his subconscious. On the outside, James was a well-adjusted member of society. Nobody suspected that inside, James was dying.

His nights were spent drinking himself into a stupor. When alcohol didn't cut it, his need to escape ascended to higher levels. He sought comfort and release in drugs. Cocaine being his preferred method. He was arrested twice. Jailed. Released on bail from his father. Had three driving under the influence tickets. Then became involved with a questionable woman.

Every time I'd tried to talk to James about what was going on, he'd laugh it off. However, there were moments, glimpses here and there, when James was honest and knew he was in trouble. He'd say things like, *"Do you think God has it out for me?"* He blamed society. *"Cops should be out catching murderers, not drunk drivers."* He questioned his worth. *"Why does this keep happening to me?"*

Despite three interventions and four stints in sober living facilities, James wouldn't stray from his addictions. They were the only way he wouldn't hear the negative self-talk that permeated his mind. It was a debilitating condition.

James had further to fall.

One night, the woman he'd been seeing had her daughter over to his house. Nobody knows for sure what happened except those three, but James was arrested for child molestation.

He was high and drunk at the time of the incident. Three years of court drama later, James was sentenced to ten years in prison for child molestation and endangerment.
Certainly an extreme case, but self-talk is powerful and can play a role in your life whether or not you choose to believe it.

CHRISSY

Chrissy was a saleswoman. A darn good one too. She grew up upper middle class, had a self-described perfectly happy upbringing, and was college educated. In her early twenties, she fell in with a crowd of, as she put it, *"Deadheads."*

She wore Grateful Dead or tie-dye t-shirts, ripped blue jeans, listened to them while she fell asleep, followed them on tours all over the country during the 1980s, and got high and drank with their followers. She did as little work as possible, and even moved to Brazil to flee her parents' lectures on her lifestyle, teaching English abroad.

She'd teach during the day, slip into a liquor shop at night and buy a huge bottle of wine, drinking it out of a paper bag while she walked home to her then boyfriend.
The pattern continued until she'd returned to the U.S. and became pregnant accidently.

Talking to her today, when I asked what made her change to a clean, sober life, she instantly replied:

"I knew I was an addict. I think all addicts know they have addictive personalities. For some people it's shopping, some its cars, food, pot, booze, cocaine, whatever it is, even video games.

An addict will always be an addict. The choice you face as an addict is what do you want to be addicted to? For me, I wanted to be addicted to my son. My life became his." She shrugged then, eyes wistfully tearing up. *"It's been 8 years now since I've been sober.*

I don't put myself in a position where I know alcohol may be involved. It's just not something I want to be around anymore. I volunteer for alcoholics' anonymous call-in line once every other week and still attend A.A. meetings. It reminds me of who I was before, who I am now, and who I want to be tomorrow.

But, as I've aged, I've also realized that my son, who's now 7 years old, is depending on me less and less. I've found healthier outlets for my addiction. I've taken up cooking because I had to learn how to cook to feed my son, but now I'm really good at it. And yoga."

Chrissy and James were a lot alike. If they'd known each other in real life, I'm sure they would've been fast friends during their heyday. The difference is Chrissy made a choice to overcome her fears and focus on a positive, fulfilling life.

While James continued to bemoan himself all the way through his trial. He went so far as to blame his boss and co-workers for landing him in jail even though they had nothing to do with it.

Both of them had doubts and negative self-talk to lead them on a journey that ultimately would become the rest of their lives. What if you could change all that? What if the negative self-talk that infiltrates your mind could be reduced, or erased?

Is it possible?
It is.
Change is closer than you think.
The negative voice in your head can be questioned and ultimately, controlled.

Chapter 1- Changing Your Story

Many years ago I attended a workshop called Landmark Education. If you've never heard of it, Landmark is an intense, three or four day workshop, lasting from nine a.m. to ten in the evening every day.

Aside from the more spiritual aspects of the seminar, I'll discuss a more psychological perspective that literally changed my life and the way I think about situations.

COLORED LENSES

As a group, we tend to believe we're open minded, objective, willing to listen to the other person's perspective. It's the biggest lie. We see the world the way we want it to be. We want it to make sense to us. Our minds are defaulted to a logical order where we can place concepts, ideas, people, and their actions into baskets. It's a definitive, if limiting way to view life.

During conversation, we're constantly analyzing, scrutinizing, and evaluating our own dialogue and those of the people we're conversing with. It's a never-ending process of judgment.

For example, I was talking to a friend who's in his mid-thirties, let's call him Ron, about an incident at their place of employment. The company has no formal dress code. Ron was wearing khakis, and a colored, short sleeved collared shirt which was untucked, and dress shoes.

Not unlike anything any other employee had worn on a typical day at the office. In the afternoon, Ron's superior approached him and chided him for wearing his shirt untucked and ended the conversation with, "you could clean up a little bit."

No other employee had received any chastisement and, to make matters worse and infuriated Ron, the very person who was lecturing him about unprofessionalism with untucked shirts was wearing a Tommy Bahama shirt, untucked.

Ron worked himself into a lather over this incident, resenting the fact that he was singled out. Additionally, he was galled that his superior had the tenacity to reprimand Ron when he was guilty of the same conduct.

What did Ron do to appease himself? He told himself a story to explain the situation in a way that made sense to him.

"*You know my boss is older,*" he said to me, nodding. "*Getting near seventy. It's a generational thing. My shirt is *designed to be worn untucked even though it has the curves and his Tommy Bahama shirt has a straight hem."* He shrugged then. *"But those older guys don't know that. If it's a post 1980 fashion trend, forget about it."*

CONTEXT

Ron's way of dealing with what had happened to him was not unusual. Whenever someone says something to us, whether positive or negative, our brains kick into overdrive. Overanalyzing every detail, nuance, and segment of the conversation.

How many times have you heard the phrase: It's not what you said, it's how you said it.

This is because our brains ruminate on everything. That we'll run ourselves ragged going in circles with questions. What did he mean by that? What made him say that? Why'd he say that?

When the answers aren't provided to us, we make them up.

He said that because he's old.

She didn't respond to my text because she hates me.

He's not calling me back because he's with another woman.

Once again, without the answers, our brains have a tendency to fill in the blanks with a barrage of negativity. We write a story around what happened to justify the encounter. We want it – no we need it to make sense in our little worlds.

I'd run into Ron again a few weeks later at a barbeque and asked him how his relationship was going with his boss. He didn't even remember the shirt incident so I'd gently reminded him.

"Oh that? It's funny, he wasn't really criticizing my shirt that day. He was actually referring to my shirt the previous day. You see the day before I'd worn a dress shirt and forgot to tuck it in when I'd returned from the bathroom.

I also had a ketchup stain on it from lunch that I didn't notice. Turns out, he just wanted me to tuck in my dress shirt because it was so long, it seemed as though I was wearing a nightgown. He wasn't wrong."

Here Ron was, agonizing for hours, maybe even days, over a two-minute conversation he'd had with his boss. It'd unnerved him so much that he'd told me the story that evening over dinner. Probably stuck with him during the night, causing him to toss and turn and giving him a restless sleep.

The story Ron concocted to explain his superior's remand turned out to be entirely false.

How much time did he waste letting his doubts and fears crush him? What opportunities were lost during this period? What if that time could have been spent spending time with his family? His wife? His children? Working on his house, completing a passion project?

Instead, he'd had a beer, gone to bed angry, and woke up exhausted from a sleepless night.

Because of the story in his head.

STOP THE FALSE STORY

Nothing in this world is good or bad, but thinking makes it so.

- **William Shakespeare**

Emotions aren't something you're attacked with. They don't jump out of you from the shadows, lurking in the corner. Nobody has a gun to your head forcing you to feel a certain way. Nobody makes you mad just the same as nobody can force you to love them.

You are responsible for your own emotions.

You are responsible for being annoyed, afraid, or insulted.

Upon the story creation, there are only two possible outcomes: confront them head-on, or fall victim to them.

What does that mean?

It means that you can be a protagonist, mastering your emotions, or you can be antagonist and preyed upon by your own mind. Will you let your fears run wild? Imagining the worst possible scenarios? Or will you find an alternative, logical and rational explanation?

Ron created a story to explain the why, how, and what of his superior's actions.

And it was all wrong!

Because a story aren't the facts. They are our mind's way of explaining the gaps in our knowledge.

Ron felt attacked, singled out. He thought, "How am I supposed to judge my reprimand? Why am I the one who's being picked on?" He justified it by diminishing his superior and practiced a form of ageism. This made Ron feel better about himself.

We're always telling ourselves stories. It's so fast, most don't even notice they're doing it.

Someone cut me off on the road, he's a jerk!

Someone laughed at me, so I got angry because I don't like being made fun of.

I was fired at work because my boss hates me. Let's sue!

These are simple, every day examples of how often we tell stories to ourselves to explain encounters in our everyday life.

Perhaps the other driver didn't see you because you were in his blind spot.

What if the person laughing wasn't even laughing at you but remembering something that made them chuckle?

What if you were fired not because your boss hates you, but because you were legitimately underperforming?

MASTER THE STORY

Stories can be mastered to stop the negative self-talk that so quickly consumes us. There are simple, and effective ways to counteract this process. I must warn you, it's difficult. It requires self-evaluation and eventually, self-realization.

Stories happen in the blink of an eye. Sometimes we're aware of them, other times, we're not until it's too late.

First, you must slow down.

That's right. Take a breath. A long inhale through the nose and an even longer exhale. Notice the way your body feels. Ask yourself if you're tense? Uptight? Flexing any of your muscles involuntarily?

Pay attention to your behavior. Are you fidgeting? Is your gaze bouncing off the walls? Is your foot tapping? Are you anxious? What words are you using in your speech? Are they short, angry sentences? A form of violence.

Or are you clamming up? Arms crossed over your chest in a huff of consternation? Silence is another form of protest, a form of aggression.

Once you've acknowledged your behavior, physically and from your speech and language being used, ask yourself, what emotions are causing this?

Do you feel hurt? Scared? Attacked? Put upon? Embarrassed? Ignored?

Next, analyze the stories that fuel these emotions. What are you telling yourself to justify the way you're acting and feeling?

And finally, question your story. What evidence do you have to support it? Find out the facts. Don't let your negative mind fill in those gaps! If you're talking to someone who's sparked a reaction in you, ask them to clarify what they meant when they said what they had.

It's not your job to interpret someone's body language – he scoffed so I know he doesn't value my opinion. He could've scoffed for a variety of reasons. You don't know for a fact why he behaved the way he did until you ask.

I know my boss hates me because he doesn't say hi to me every morning.

Clue: If you can see or hear something, is it a fact or a behavior?

Likely a behavior which you are attaching a story to so that you can explain it.

Clarity is greater than ambiguity. Verifiable objectivity trumps observation.

Chapter 2- Time Out

We are personable creatures. Our reality is based upon our senses: sight, hearing, touch, taste, smell. Without those objective forms of experience, we don't know something for sure. Once we have those aspects from which to draw a conclusion, it becomes personal. For instance, it's more difficult to imagine something without having experienced it.

A vacation to Hawaii doesn't become real until you're there, standing on the shores of the Black Sand beach in Maui.

The promotion at work doesn't seem possible until you get the raise and see the money in your bank account.

Cancer doesn't hit home until someone you love is diagnosed with it.

When you find a tough situation is thrust upon you, you'll immediately dive into your story. And, as discussed in the previous chapter, we've covered some exercises to help create a new story.

However, here are some alternative methods used to combat the negative self-talk that rears its ugly head from time to time.

DETACH YOURSELF

Imagine that you weren't the one going through this. What if it was a friend? A colleague? A family member?

How would you counsel them? What would you say to alleviate their fears and to bring them back to a rational, even logical way of looking at things? Hot headed tempers sprout up fast, burning deep within us. How would you calm your friend down?

Taking a third party, observer point-of-view detaches you from the personal connection you have with a situation. It's no longer happening to you. You'll be able to see it from another angle and think creatively about how to tackle the issue.

REFRAME

Many years ago my friend Andrew was involved in a car accident. Fortunately, nobody was injured and everyone was relatively safe with minor cuts and bruises. But it was a total wreck. The vehicle couldn't be salvaged.

"Oh no," I'd said. "Didn't you just buy that car last year?"

"*Yup.*"

I could tell he was broken up. Nursing a beer in his hand, gaze cast towards the lawn. He wasn't having any fun at his daughter's birthday party. Instead, he was racking up the bills he'd have to pay and feared a lawsuit by the passenger's in the other vehicle.

"*At least you get a new car,*" I'd said.

He paused. Mulling over my statement.

"*Insurance does cover it,*" he let slip, twisting his mouth into a knot.

"*Yeah. The only question is what are you going to buy now!*" I said.

Suddenly a grin stretched across his face and he was talking about the new vehicles he saw while he drove by the dealership the other day. He became so excited about the idea he wanted to hop on the internet and peruse cars that minute.

"My life has been filled with terrible misfortunes, most of which have never happened."

- Mark Twain

Reframing is when we take a situation, usually misfortunate, and spin it to form a positive outcome. It's a process that's been used for decades. Because we're bombarded by negativity and terrifying possible scenarios that could happen to us, reframing becomes a valuable technique.

 Anything that doesn't contribute positively to the situation must be discarded in favor of thoughts that do.

It's important to keep in mind our stories.

Events do not have any meaning.

We assign meaning and value to them as a result of our stories. What story do you want to ascribe to a life event? Something horrendous? Or, alternatively, something fabulous?

Every idea, thought, or belief you have comes attached with a frame.

James believed he was never good enough for his parents to accept him so he found solace in drugs.

Ron felt he was being picked on by his superior for a perfectly acceptable office attire.

Chrissy reframed her life to focus on her son.

Whatever your assumptions are become your frame of reference.

Reframing takes two steps: identify the negative thought and substitute it with a positive one.

SUBSTITUTING NEGATIVE THOUGHTS

Don't kid yourself. Identifying negative thoughts is a daunting task. It's filled with fright and peril. Often we don't want to be self-critical. It hurts. We feel raw, exposed, and vulnerable. Subject to injury.

But a whole world awaits if you can accomplish this. Step by step, little by little. Learn to know yourself, understand how you think, and what drives you to leap to those undesirable conclusions.

Once identified, how do we accomplish the task of substituting negativity for positivity?

1. Identify and replace harsh language.

Words matter. Thoughts matter. They have weight and value or else we wouldn't be hurt by them. The old adage of "sticks and stones may break my bones but words will never hurt me" was a dangerous lie. If you're constantly telling yourself that you're worthless, you'll believe it.

Use softer language. Instead, say that you have weaknesses which could be worked on.

2. Find the best solution.

When Andrew had the wreck, his attention was devoted to the problems it caused. In lieu of directing your energies to the problems, cultivate your time in searching for a solution.

3. Discover a lesson.

There's a lesson in everything life has to offer. It's no one's job but yours to find it. Seek that and you'll find peace. Last year I'd met a friend who was laid off from work.
Instead of wallowing in her loss, she sought the freedom not having a job entailed. A year later, she's the proud owner of a Pilates studio and following her passion.

4. Question assumptions.

Most of our stories are derived from our preconceived notions about people, events, or situations. Stories wrapped up in more stories. Like discussed in the section entitled Mastering

Your Story, we must always be vigilant and challenge our assumptions.

They don't lead to the truth. Discover reasons why you believe what you do. Chase the origination of those negative thoughts. Go where others won't dare to in their psyche.

Chapter 3- The Placebo Effect

Modern medicine is riddled with phenomenon. Stories of miraculous recoveries that befuddle both doctors and patients alike. Most of these are random acts of luck, some of the more devoted attribute inexplicable recoveries to God or another form of divine intervention. Yet there is a third component to these cases.

The Placebo Effect.

Doctors can be still up in the air about the true merit of the Placebo response, however, time after time, study after study, it has proven that it is a legitimate psychological phenomenon.

What is the Placebo Effect?

Put simply, the Placebo Effect is when patients are given a fake treatment, typically an inactive substance (like a sugar pill or injected with a saline solution) rather than real medicine. And, viola, seemingly through a miracle, the patient is cured of their illness.

How can this be?

The mind has cured them.

Psychology can be an all powerful tool for the sick and ill. Sometimes, when a patient wants to believe that a medicine cured them, even if it wasn't a legitimate treatment, the mind makes it so and produces physiological changes within the body that can be measured.

In short, the Placebo Effect is a self-fulfilling prophecy. You have a headache, a doctor gives you a sugar pill, and you feel as though it helped you, so therefore, because your brain wills it to be, your body adapts.

In 2014, the New England Journal of Medicine published a finding that a fake surgery can have the same effects as the real thing. The study was conducted by surgeons from Finland on those who'd suffered from a torn meniscus and required knee surgery.

One group was given the true surgery and the other, a fake surgery. The surgeons pretended to pass around surgical instruments in the operating room, made slight incisions to replicate the evidence of a surgery. For all intents and purposes, the patients who received the fake surgery never even knew they weren't operated on.

Months later the surgeons followed up with both groups, the ones who'd received the real surgery and those who'd received the fake.

Both groups reported an increase in agility and flexibility, decrease pain, and an overall successful surgery.

But how could this be if fully half of the patients never even had a surgery but were tricked?

The mind.

They wanted to believe the surgery worked and therefore it did.

Before the year 2000, most in the medical community thought the Placebo Effect was only useful when it came to pills or injections. Now, however, we know that the mind can have a bigger impact than we believed, extending into surgeries.

If your mind wants it to be so, it will produce the changes in your body to make it so.

From the Doctor's Chair

Timothy Wilson, Ph.D., Professor of Psychology at the University of Virginia, wrote a book entitled Redirect: The Surprising New Science of Psychological Change.

In it, he postulates that stories create our reality. Negative self-talk pollutes and distorts our version of true events. Assigning false meanings and leading down dangerous corridors of self-doubt, pity, and self-righteous consternation.

During times of extreme frustration, lack of motivation, and depression, Mr. Wilson advocates the use of writing therapy. A type of process which utilizes the process and creativity of writing to lessen and delve into darker emotional territory.

First developed by social psychologist James Pennebaker, Ph.D., a psychologist from the University of Texas, Austin, writing therapy is a way to extrapolate feelings which we didn't know we had buried.

Initial studies had simple processes and rules. Write until the allotted time is up and don't worry about spelling, punctuation, or grammar. Mr. Pennebaker was clear that the participates had to write about their darkest, deepest, most vulnerable feelings about a particularly traumatic incident which had occurred to them.

Two groups were formed: the emotional group and objective, or control, group. Rather than write about their feelings of trauma, the control group was instructed to write factually about their plans for the day. Expressly forbidding them to discuss topics of opinion, emotion, or feelings.

Though the study lasted only four days in the 1980s, it spawned over two hundred subsequent studies because they'd found that the group who wrote about their emotions related to trauma had significantly fewer visits to the doctors than in the past.

In Timothy Wilson's book, he advises that those who experience such negativity in their life, who's natural predisposition is to bombard themselves with negative self-talk, causing them anxiety, depression, and anger, to try this exercise.

Grab a piece of paper and a pen or pencil. For fifteen minutes before bed, begin writing about what's troubling you. It sounds simple but isn't. Often we're unwilling to truly get to the heart of the matter, preferring superficial answers to our dilemmas. Never probing further.

Being real hurts. Being raw, open, and exposed leaves us feeling vulnerable. Even if we're only admitting fragility to ourselves. We're the last to admit we need help. We want to be proud, we want to be strong. Impervious to pain.

This isn't reality.

As an exercise, this is incredibly beneficial. Mr. Wilson says that in the beginning, you might be writing in a jumble, an incoherent stream of consciousness. Leaping from one random subject to the next without rhyme, reason, consistency, or logic behind it. This isn't unusual. It's natural. He actually says that those who start this way typically receive the biggest benefits from the exercise.

It's something that can be done before bed, during lunch, after dinner, or on a coffee break at work. You can also use a computer, laptop, or any other device where you can type quickly, without editing or hitting the wrong keys.

After four days have elapsed most find a new narrative to the event in question. A new meaning, a new way of looking at the situation. This perspective shift allows you to stop ruminating on it, twisting and turning your way into a downward spiral of negativity. The gnawing feeling that claws in your gut, that makes it hard to breath, which weighs you down night after night will have lightened.

The Way Forward

Every one of us has a story to tell. Every one of us has known someone who's view of life has led them down a dark path. Whether that is drugs, alcohol, partying, financial irresponsibility, or other forms of reckless behavior, our minds have the ultimate control over our fate. It is up to us to determine how we live our lives, what story we write for ourselves, what our future holds.

Wallowing over the tragedies that befall us, whether real or perceived, leads us nowhere. Stewing on events that seem to be out of our control, fanatical about every last detail of what someone said, how they said it, what their body language was, what their facial expression conveyed, neither propels us in a positive, forward-thinking direction nor helps us achieve peace.

Vigilance is the answer.

I'm reminded of a quote from Mahatma Ghandi:

> *"Your beliefs become your thoughts,*
> *Your thoughts become your words,*

Your words become your actions,
Your actions become your habits,
Your habits become your values,
Your values become your destiny."

What we allow in our minds is what we allow escape our lips. We constantly say things we regret later. Usually these things are said in the heat of the moment, when we're fuming mad, ready to reign hellfire down upon the world. And we're upset because we're hurt, betrayed, or judged. When attacked, we return the volley tenfold.

None of those actions are the answer. During those crucial moments, tense conversations, heated exchanges, fights, and arguments, that is the clearest time for vigilance. Combat the negative self-talk which is likely to surface. Be on guard for it.

Use the techniques in this book to counteract our natural tendencies before they consume us. We are good, born in the light, if we choose to be. Choose that path.

Made in the USA
San Bernardino, CA
15 June 2016